MW01097359
MASTERS
OF THE UNIVERSE

MASTERS
OF THE UNIVERSE

WHAT WOULD SKELETOR DO?

WHAT WOULD SKELETOR DO?

Diabolical Ways to Master the Universe

ROBB PEARLMAN

UNIVERSE

First published in the United States of America in 2019 by
Universe Publishing
A Division of Rizzoli International Publications, Inc.
300 Park Avenue South
New York, NY 10010
www.rizzoliusa.com

Design by Lynne Yeamans
Retouching by Molly Dauphin

Contents

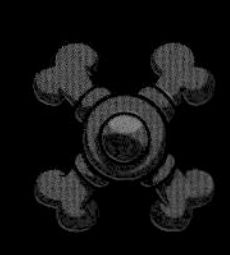

Preface

BY ROBB PEARLMAN

I know I'm supposed to be 100% behind He-Man, Heroic Warrior and Prince of Eternia, but I can't help admire his chief rival, Skeletor. No matter how many times his evil schemes to overthrow King Randor are stopped by He-Man and his friends, or his quest to invade Castle Grayskull is thwarted by Eternian magic or his own hubris, Skeletor never, never, never gives up. He's practically Churchilian, and that's admirable in its own way. Evil and wrongheaded and reprehensible, but admirable nonetheless.

Skeletor may be misguided (and evil–he's definitely evil), but I think the lessons offered in this book can serve as a starting-off point for you to apply his singular brand of stick-to-itiveness to your own life.

But don't do what he does. Or think what he thinks. Because he's evil.

—R.P.

Foreword

BY SKELETOR

I could write a book about what you don't know! So why do I only get a foreword in a book that's about me?

Because the only things more powerful than the spells that protect Castle Grayskull are the clauses in a publishing contract. And, as if that wasn't enough, thanks to Beast Man, Eternia's worst lawyer, I'm trapped in the unbreakable bonds of a Non-Disclosure Agreement so I can't even tell you exactly how I feel about the royalty! J.D. doesn't stand for Juris Doctor, it stands for Just Dum-Dum!

Read this book if you must, but let me tell you, this Pearl-Man has a grain of sand for a brain. Where are the transcriptions of my most evil spells? What happened to the tales of my stunning victories? I've seen better writing on the walls of ancient ruins—and those are in hieroglyphics! He does have good grammar, though, I'll give him that much. That much, but no more!

So go ahead. Try to emulate my magnificence. You'll be even sorrier than you are now.

—Skeletor

DOLTS!
HALF-WITS!
BUNGLERS!

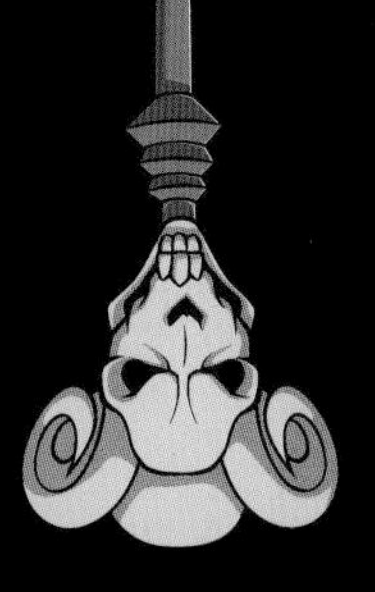

Family and Frenemies

Sometimes friends need **YOUR HELP.**

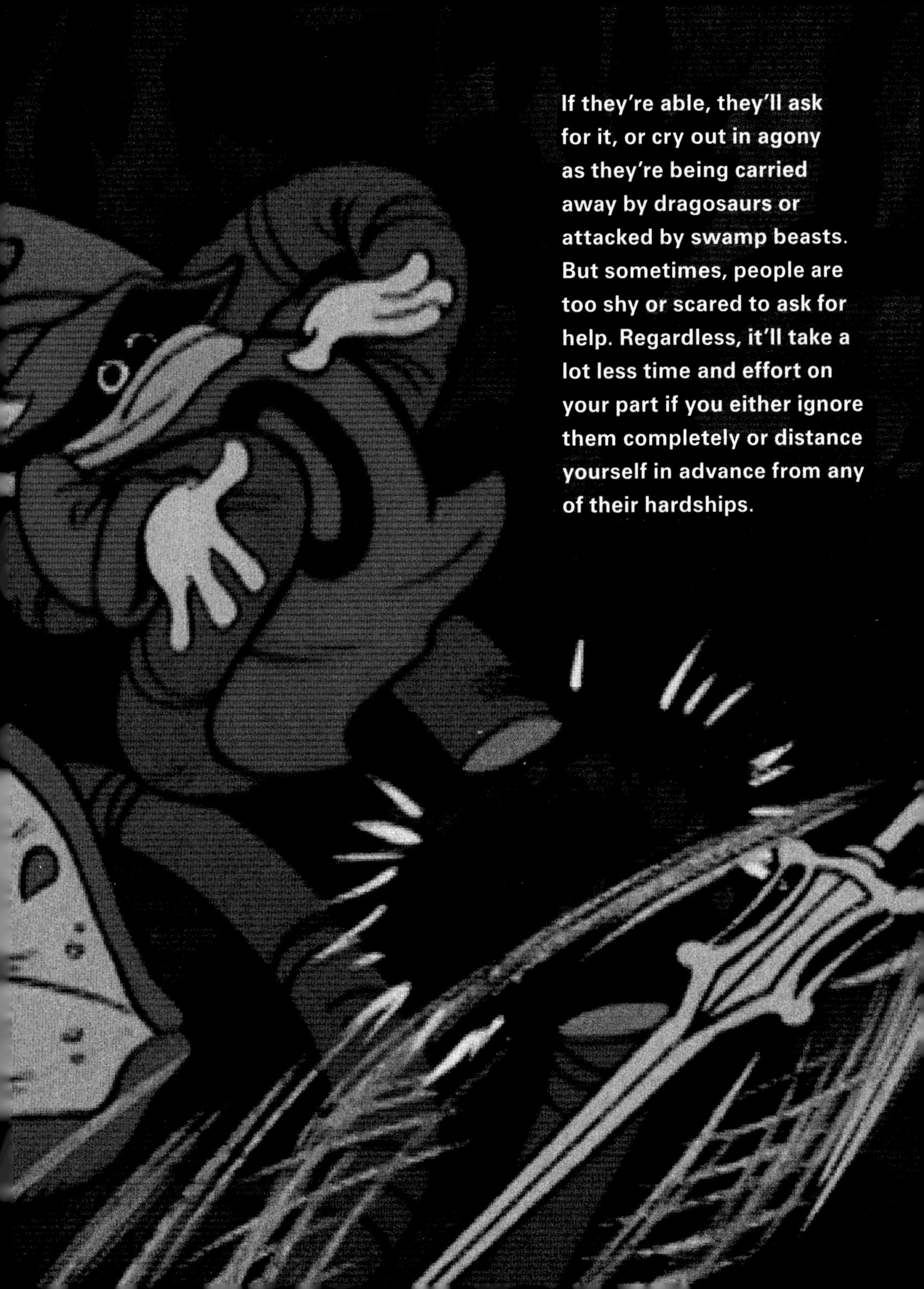

If they're able, they'll ask for it, or cry out in agony as they're being carried away by dragosaurs or attacked by swamp beasts. But sometimes, people are too shy or scared to ask for help. Regardless, it'll take a lot less time and effort on your part if you either ignore them completely or distance yourself in advance from any of their hardships.

Friends and family can offer counsel when trying to navigate life's twists and turns. It's important to listen to, and calmly consider, their suggestions. Then, after a few moments of lulling them into a sense of calm, mock them mercilessly for their nincompoopery and do what you wanted to do in the first place.

You will be judged by what you
wear–especially your shoes.
Make sure they're clean, laced up,
and always at the ready to kick
someone while they're down.

Because friends think of you as a trusted and valuable companion, they may project their feelings about something else onto you. So when they suddenly bring up long-past resentments or behave irrationally, they may be acting out because of outside influences, like a bad grade, losing an important account, or having their people enslaved by a megalomaniac. Or, they may just finally be telling you exactly what they think of you. Regardless, you didn't sign up for this. Unfriend them immediately and tell everyone how horrible they are. You'll both be glad you did.

Whether it's out to dinner, the movies, or even attending a series of never-ending open houses for properties you wish to own, spending time with friends can be great fun. As long as you're in charge. While you're on your adventure, consider the dynamics of your group. Are there only three of you? Do you notice that the other two are going off on their own, or sharing private conversations? These are all signs that you're the third wheel.

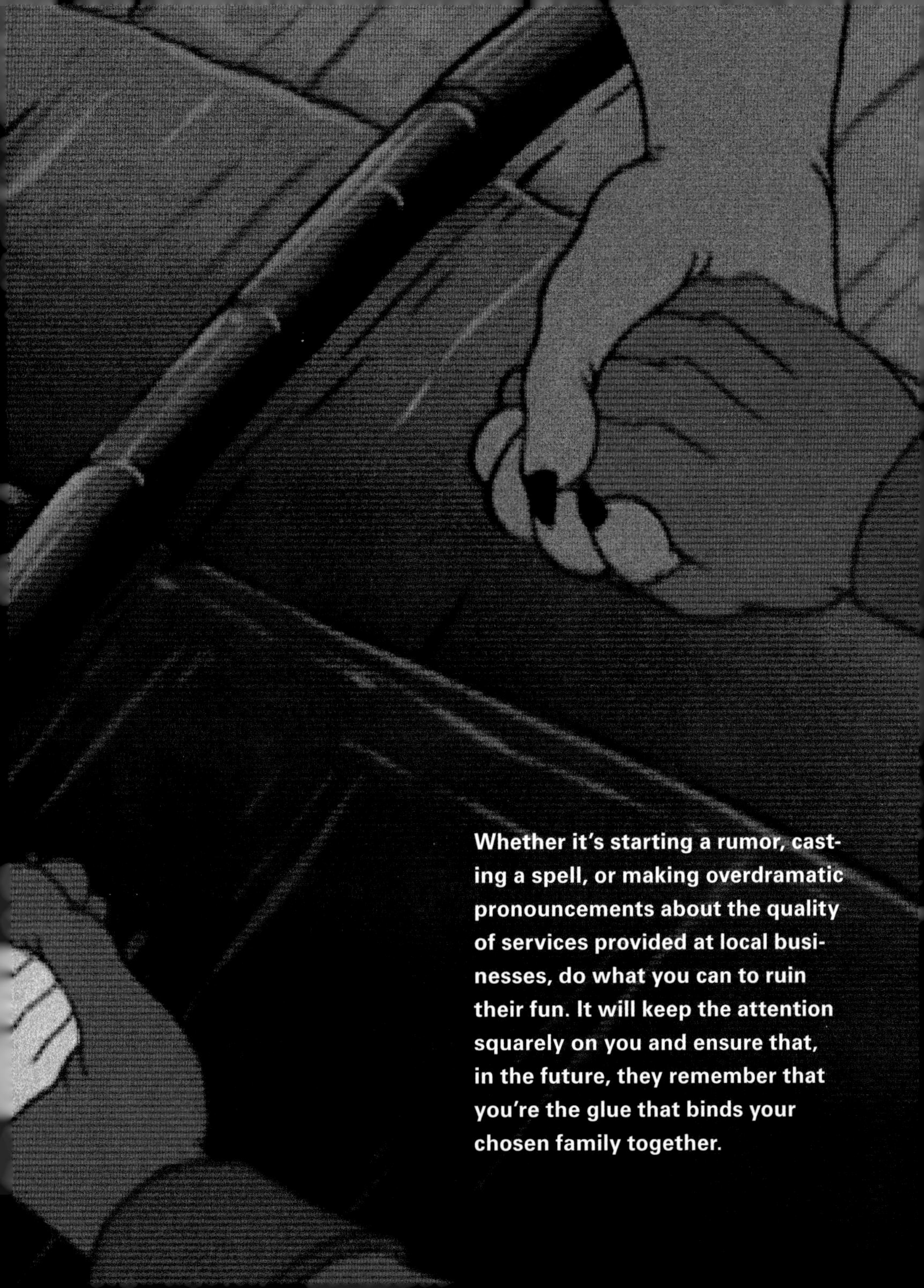

Whether it's starting a rumor, casting a spell, or making overdramatic pronouncements about the quality of services provided at local businesses, do what you can to ruin their fun. It will keep the attention squarely on you and ensure that, in the future, they remember that you're the glue that binds your chosen family together.

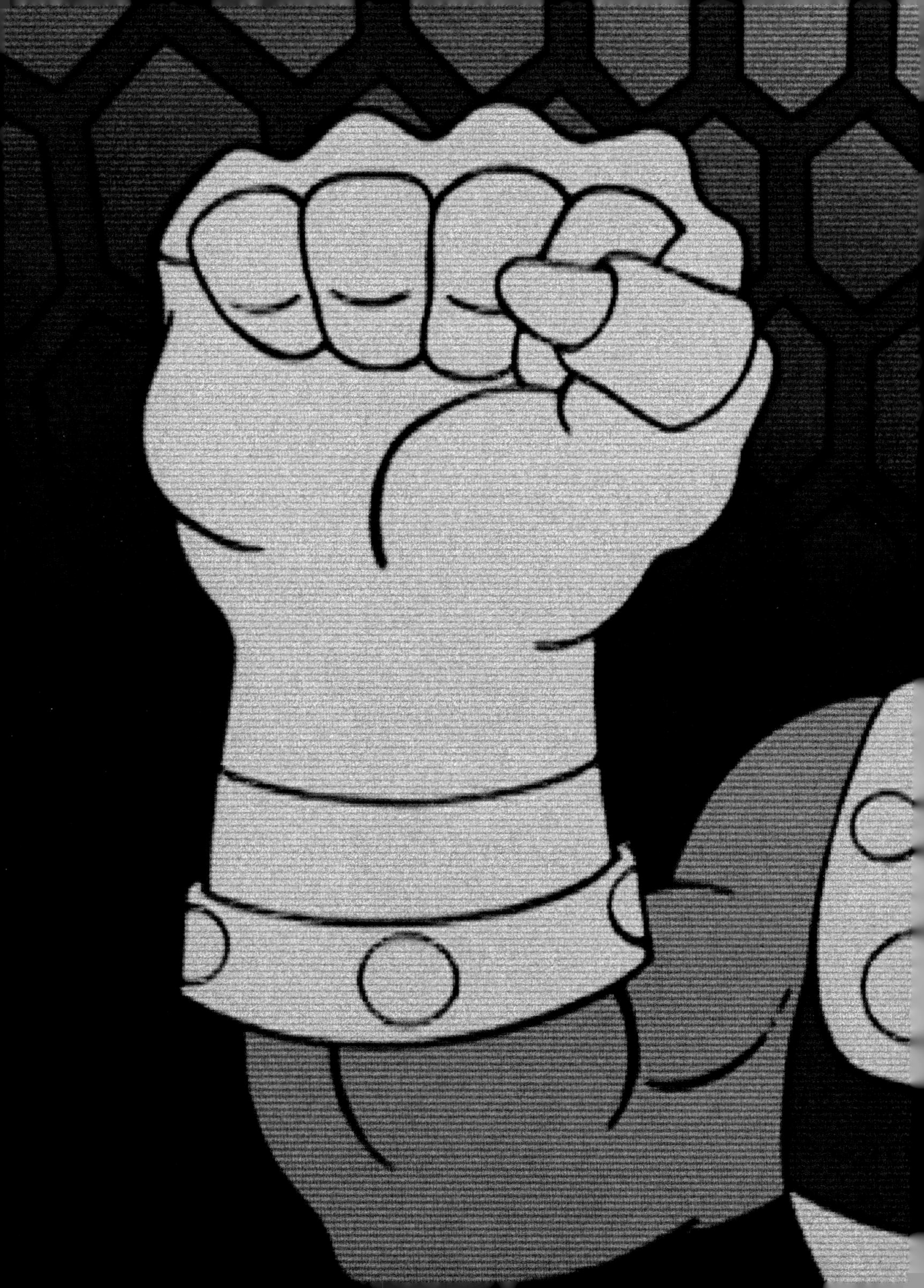

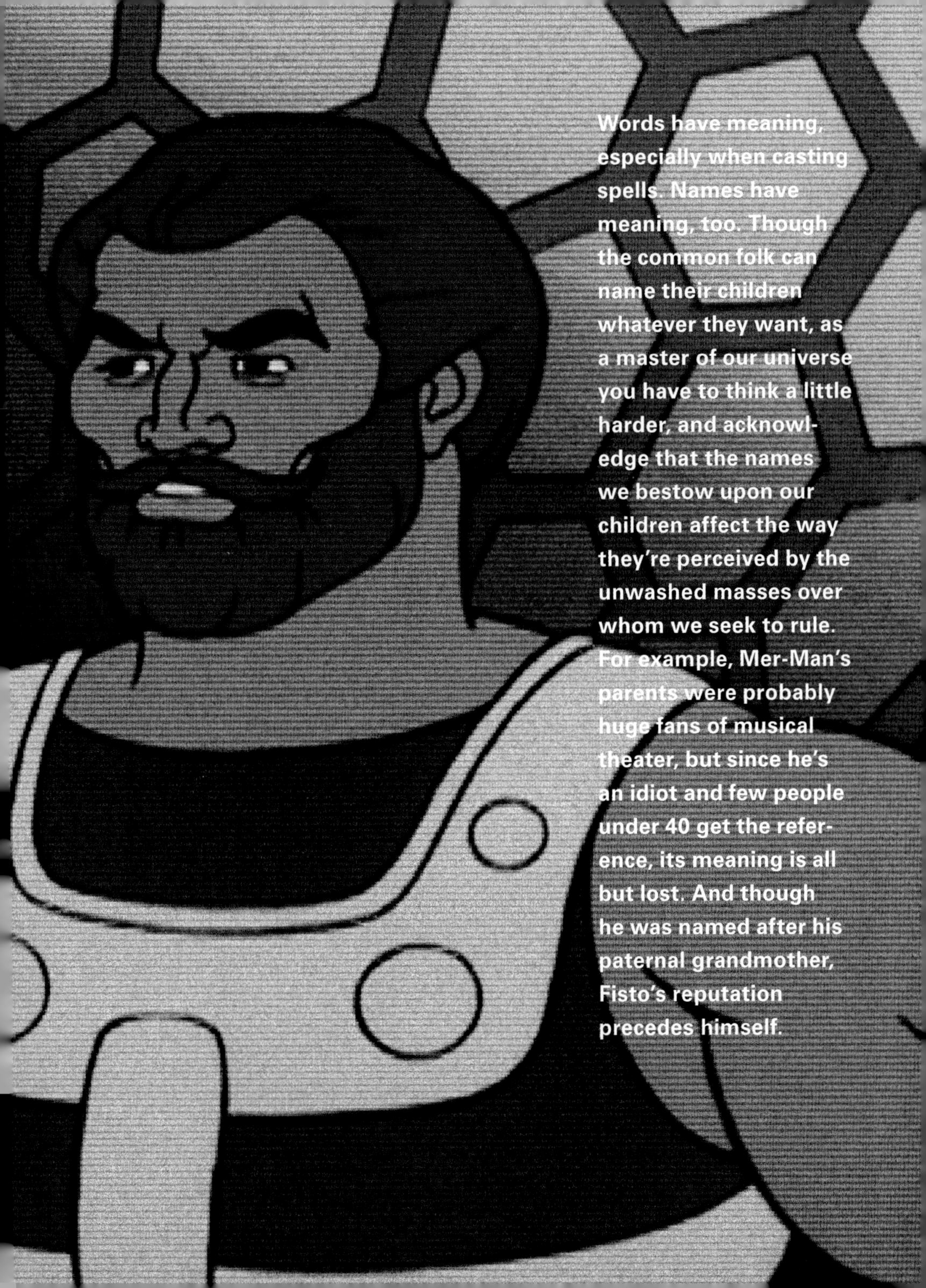

Words have meaning, especially when casting spells. Names have meaning, too. Though the common folk can name their children whatever they want, as a master of our universe you have to think a little harder, and acknowledge that the names we bestow upon our children affect the way they're perceived by the unwashed masses over whom we seek to rule. For example, Mer-Man's parents were probably huge fans of musical theater, but since he's an idiot and few people under 40 get the reference, its meaning is all but lost. And though he was named after his paternal grandmother, Fisto's reputation precedes himself.

If you
don't
have
anything
nice
to say,
say it in
a stage
whisper,

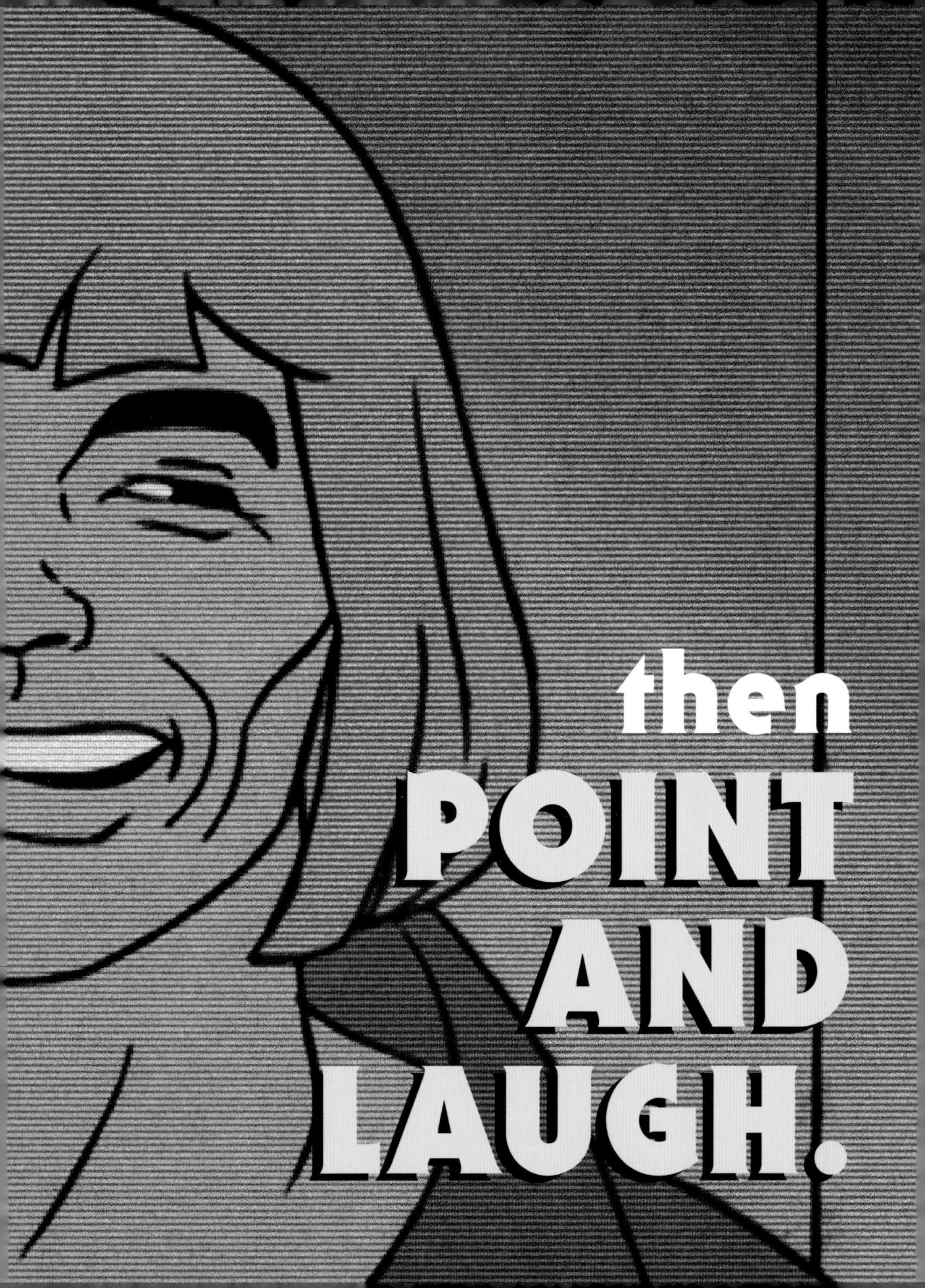

then
POINT
AND
LAUGH.

Technology is a fantastic way to keep connected, but it's rude and disrespectful to your friends and family to keep pulling out your phone or holographic projector to check for messages when you're supposed to be spending time with them. So either keep it out on the table all the time or don't accept any dinner invitations.

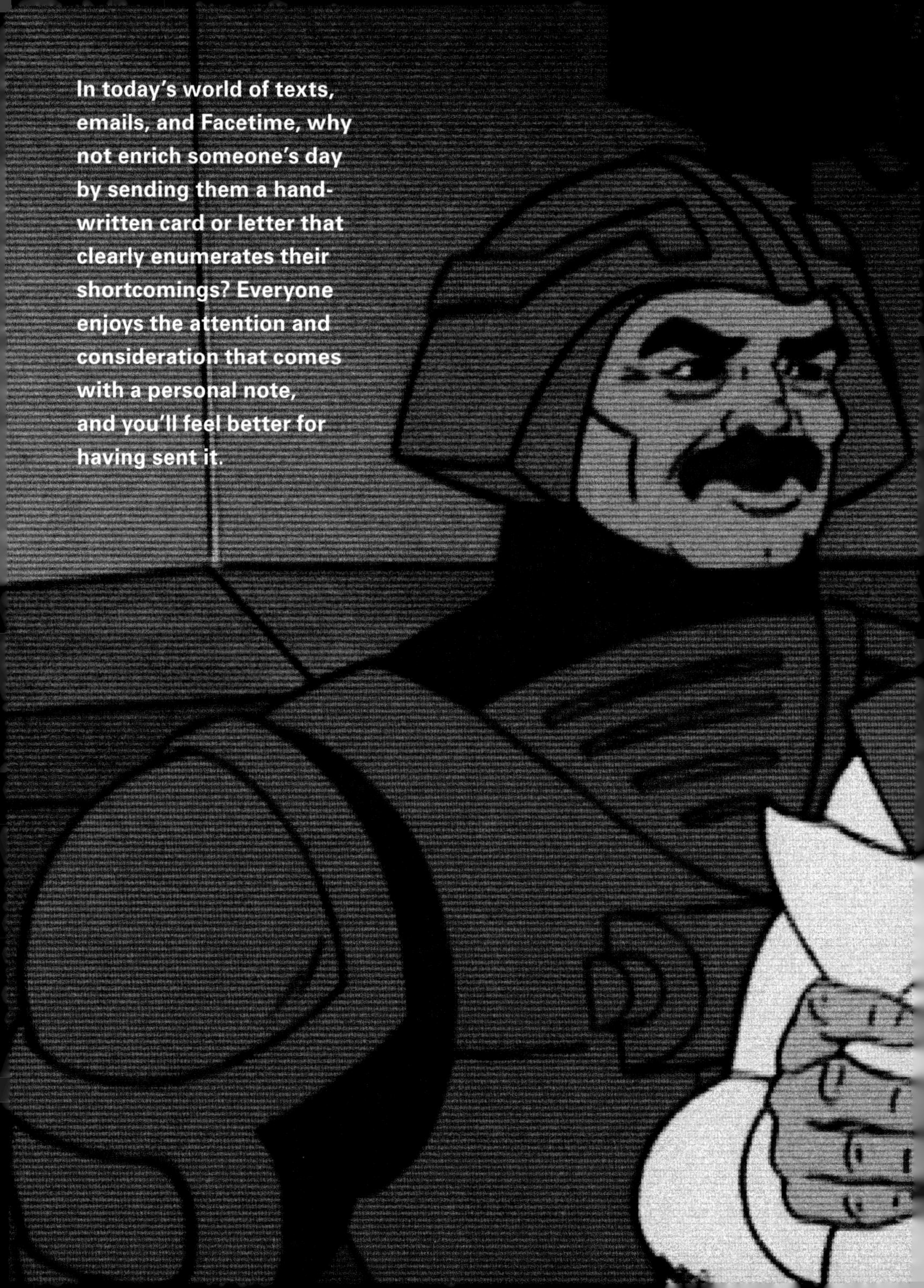

In today's world of texts, emails, and Facetime, why not enrich someone's day by sending them a hand-written card or letter that clearly enumerates their shortcomings? Everyone enjoys the attention and consideration that comes with a personal note, and you'll feel better for having sent it.

HOLIDAYS
are hard,

especially when out-of-town guests come for a visit. They disrupt your routines, put things back in the wrong place, and generally invade your personal space. Distract yourself by counting the days, hours, minutes, and seconds until they leave you in peace. When they're gone, you'll treasure those moments you had together. Especially the moment you sent them on their way.

I AM NOT NICE.
I AM NOT KIND.
AND I AM NOT
WONDERFUL.

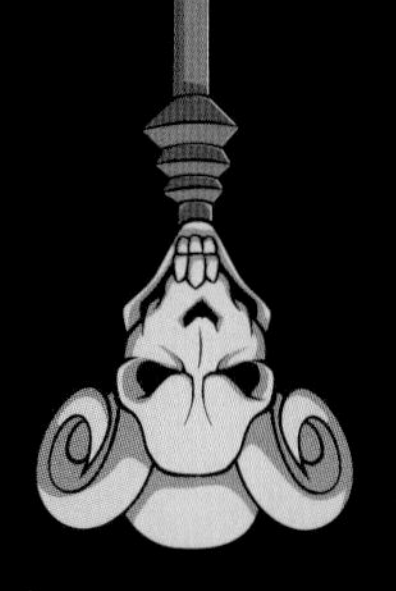

Love and Other Evils

Thinking about

a new romance?

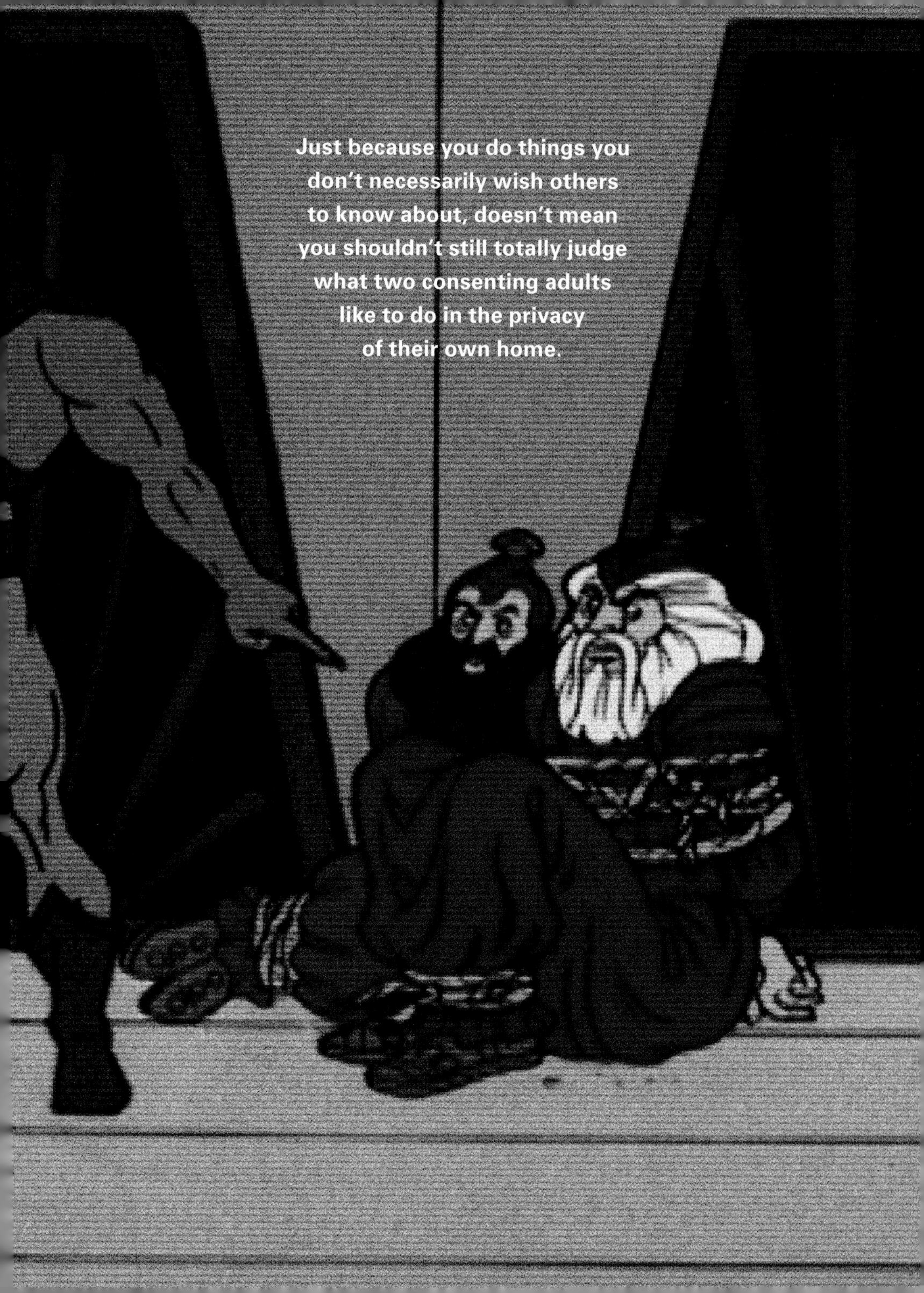
Just because you do things you
don't necessarily wish others
to know about, doesn't mean
you shouldn't still totally judge
what two consenting adults
like to do in the privacy
of their own home.

MANSPLAINING
is necessary

and usually
WELL RECEIVED.

Nobody's worth going to
JARED
for.

Sometimes we all look at a couple lovingly holding hands and think: “He got a girlfriend and I’m still single?” Rather than dwelling on the randomness of the universe and the weight of the crushing black hole of loneliness in which you find yourself, focus that rage on crushing your enemies. We all die alone, so take solace in watching them die first!

ALWAYS
leave them
wanting
MORE.

to be co

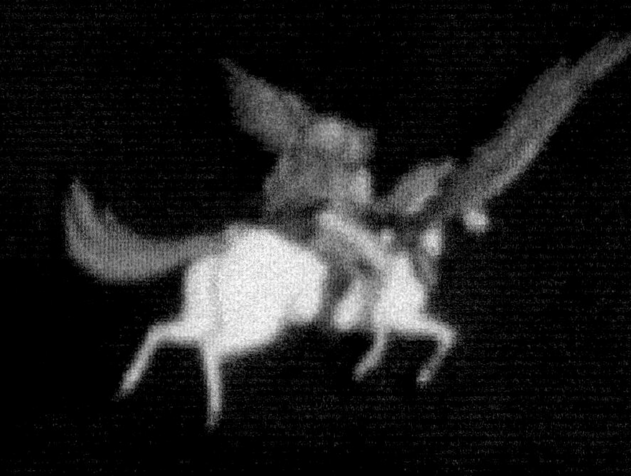

ntinued...

Things getting uncomfortable?

If you're about to get caught doing something naughty, or your significant other at a party isn't getting your "I want to leave" signal, just escape through a magic portal and leave them to their own devices.

I OUGHT TO COVER MY THRONE WITH YOUR HIDE!

Home Is Where the Hatred Is

Use a common motif around your entire home, like cold, gray stones or furniture made from the bones of your fallen foes. By creating a visual design story, you'll tie everything together, and will be noticed not only by your lackies, but by your captives as well.

Feng Shui is an ancient tradition that is intended to bring peace and harmony into your life. It's mostly Panthor poop, but when practiced correctly, it's a wonderful way to maintain magical balance—and ever-so-gently remind anyone who enters your space who's in charge.

Thinking of adopting a shelter pet?

Don't.

It will ruin your STREET CRED.

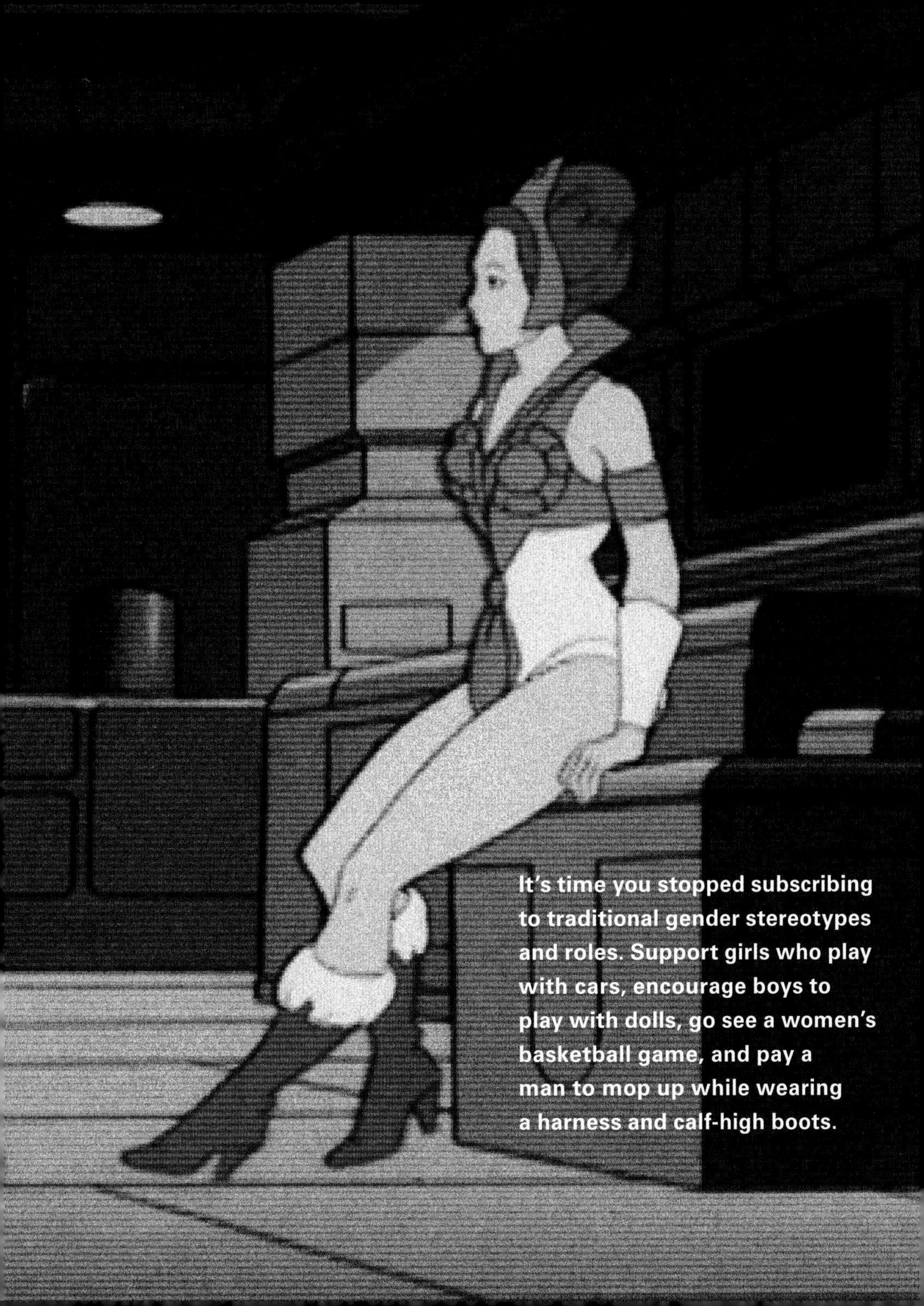

It's time you stopped subscribing to traditional gender stereotypes and roles. Support girls who play with cars, encourage boys to play with dolls, go see a women's basketball game, and pay a man to mop up while wearing a harness and calf-high boots.

Water features make excellent additions to any home.

They're relaxing and perfect for drowning your enemies.

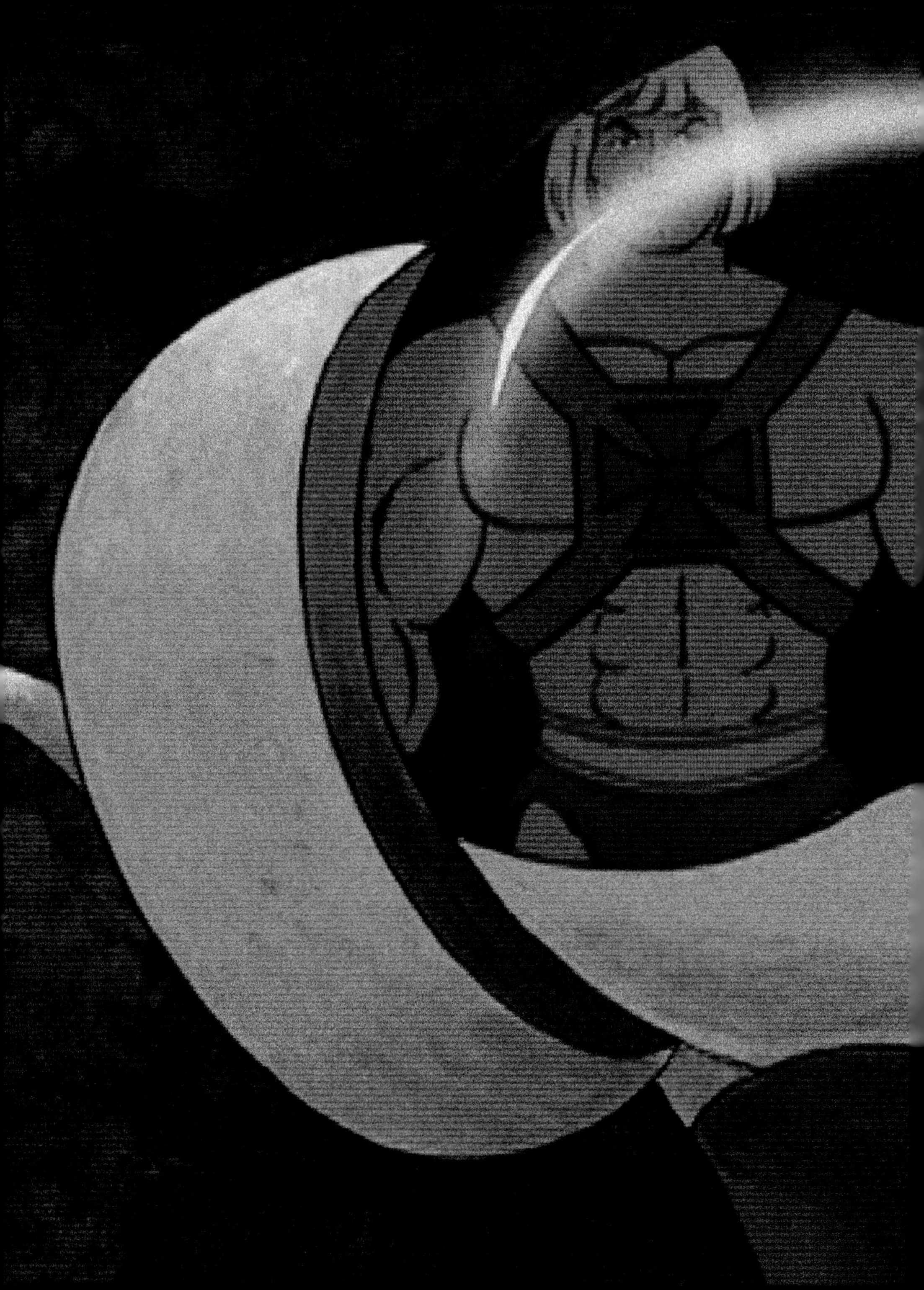

Still haven't found what you're looking for?

Check your staff! Alternatively, check your underwear drawer, your mother's purse, or the hidden corner of your soul where you lock away secrets.

WHY DO I SURROUND MYSELF WITH FOOLS?

Career

UPSET?

Shake your fists to the heavens as you curse your higher power for surrounding you with fools and miscreants—especially the ones with the flowing golden locks and happy family lives who seem to get all the breaks.

Sometimes, when you least expect it, you're going to have to rely on people you don't particularly care for. Whether it's a work project, a school science fair, or an expedition to rid your planet of invaders, we must all sometimes put aside our

differences (and, if they notice, swords) and band together for the greater good. Once your goal is accomplished, you can go back to trying to resolve your personal differences—by trying to destroy them.

Turn awkward silences to your advantage: use the time to engage in a series of exposition-laden monologues. Not only will it be informative, but it'll pass the time and continue to establish your verbal dominance over the group.

Always keep a
GLOWING
ORB
handy.

One must always blame the victim. Fools need to take a certain amount of responsibility for their actions and accept the consequences of their own stupidity. So if you're a white-collar criminal who just spent two years in a minimum-security prison for a Ponzi scheme, or if you're a sorceress based on the on-the-nose-named Isle of Tears who helped an evil troll overthrow a well-loved king by turning his army into fish people and enslaving his subjects, you're going to have to work a little harder to get people to trust you a second time. And that trust, which you so giddily discarded when it got in your way, will be a hard-earned prize once you attain it and betray it again. But most prizes are worth the time and effort, aren't they?

Always move your
face as close as
possible to the
speaker during a
CONFERENCE
CALL.

A little rebellion is a good thing. It's up to each new generation to challenge the existing status quo, push boundaries, and generally stick it to the man. Peaceful protest, letter-writing campaigns, and more artistic expressions of rebellion signal to the established ruling horde that you won't hide in your lair forever. And that you're coming for them. Soon. When they least expect it.

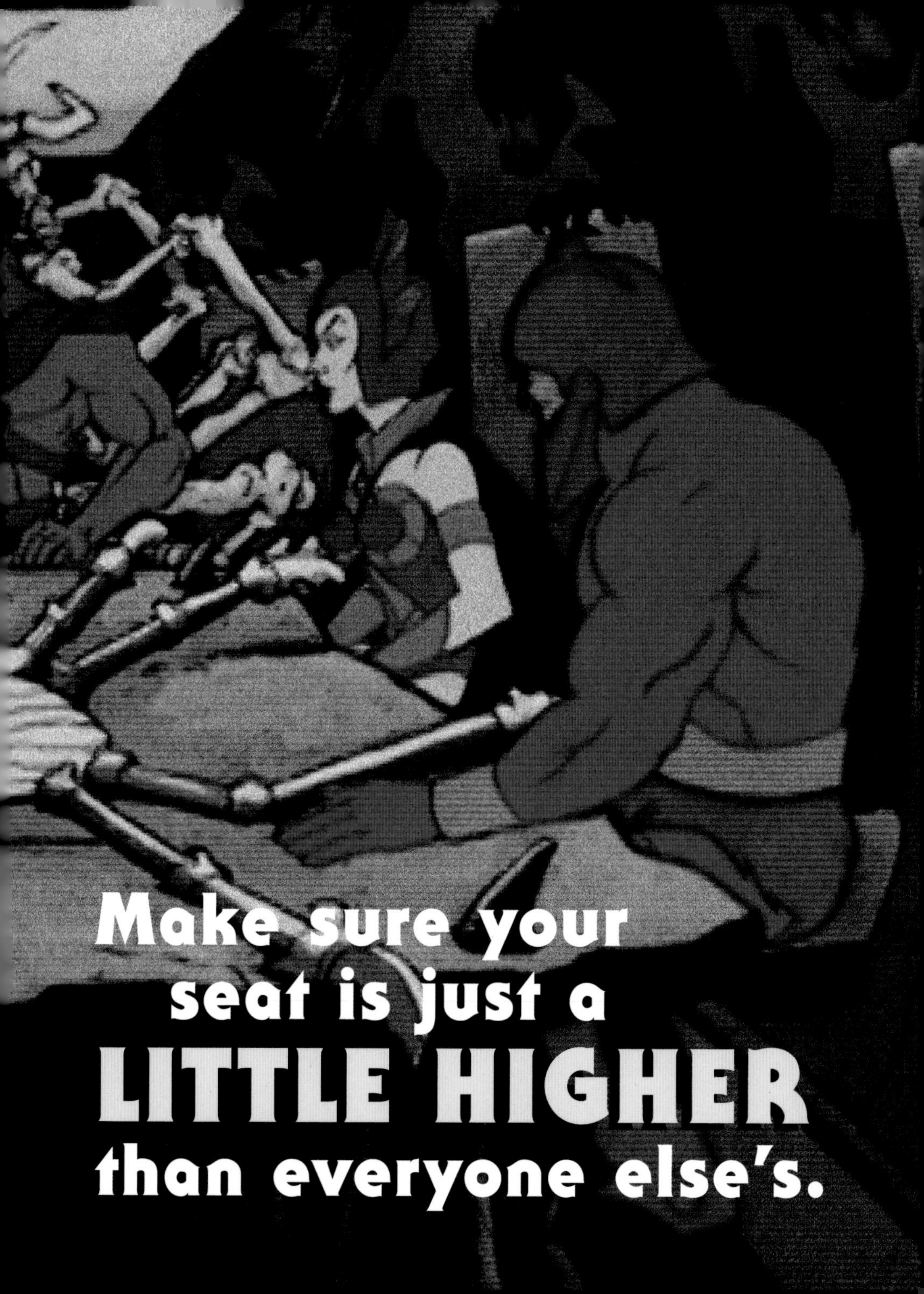
Make sure your
seat is just a
LITTLE HIGHER
than everyone else's.

YOU
ROYAL
BOOB!

Down Time

Don't
forget
about
LEG
DAY.

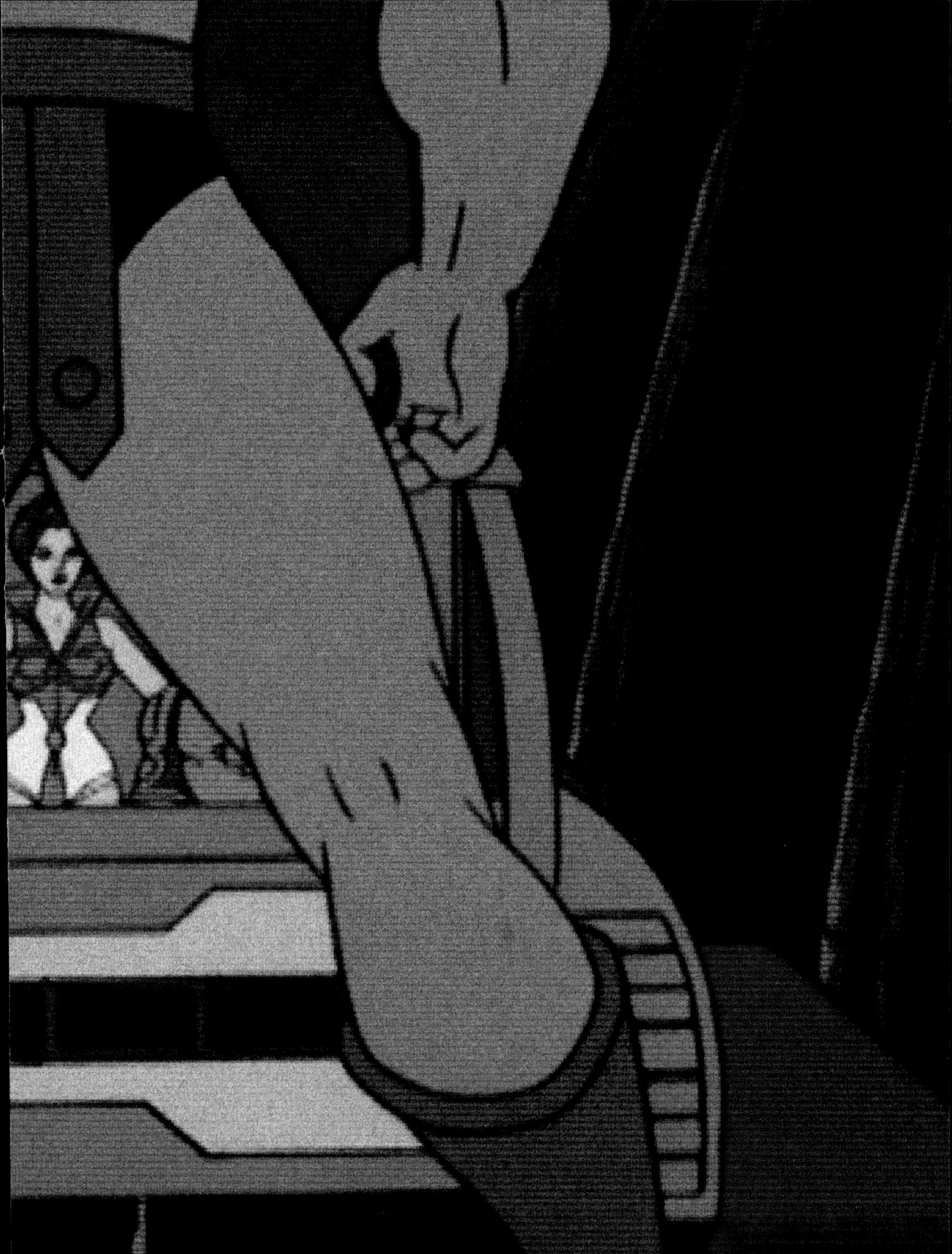

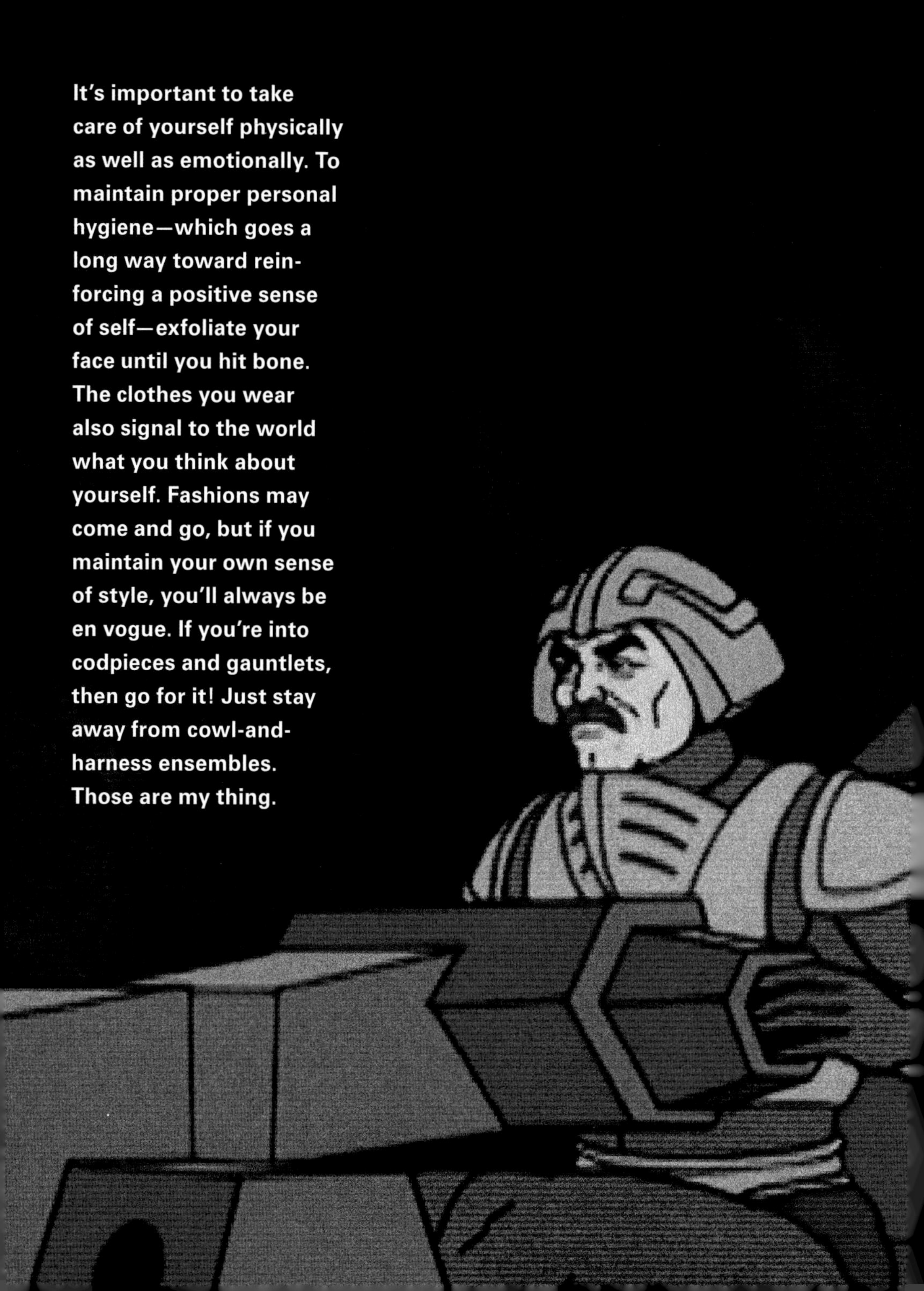

It's important to take care of yourself physically as well as emotionally. To maintain proper personal hygiene—which goes a long way toward reinforcing a positive sense of self—exfoliate your face until you hit bone. The clothes you wear also signal to the world what you think about yourself. Fashions may come and go, but if you maintain your own sense of style, you'll always be en vogue. If you're into codpieces and gauntlets, then go for it! Just stay away from cowl-and-harness ensembles. Those are my thing.

A little bit of
MANSCAPING
goes a long way.

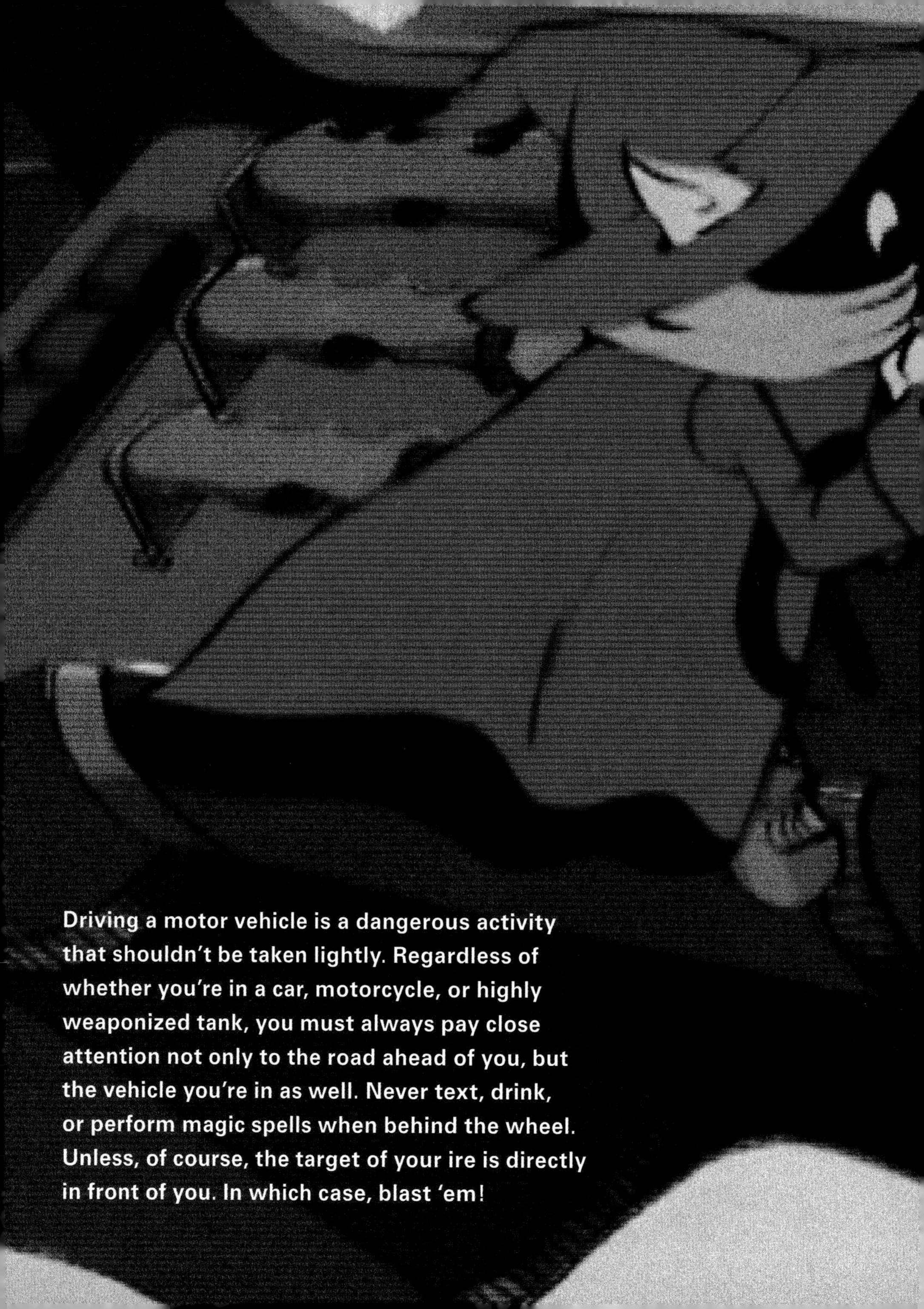

Driving a motor vehicle is a dangerous activity that shouldn't be taken lightly. Regardless of whether you're in a car, motorcycle, or highly weaponized tank, you must always pay close attention not only to the road ahead of you, but the vehicle you're in as well. Never text, drink, or perform magic spells when behind the wheel. Unless, of course, the target of your ire is directly in front of you. In which case, blast 'em!

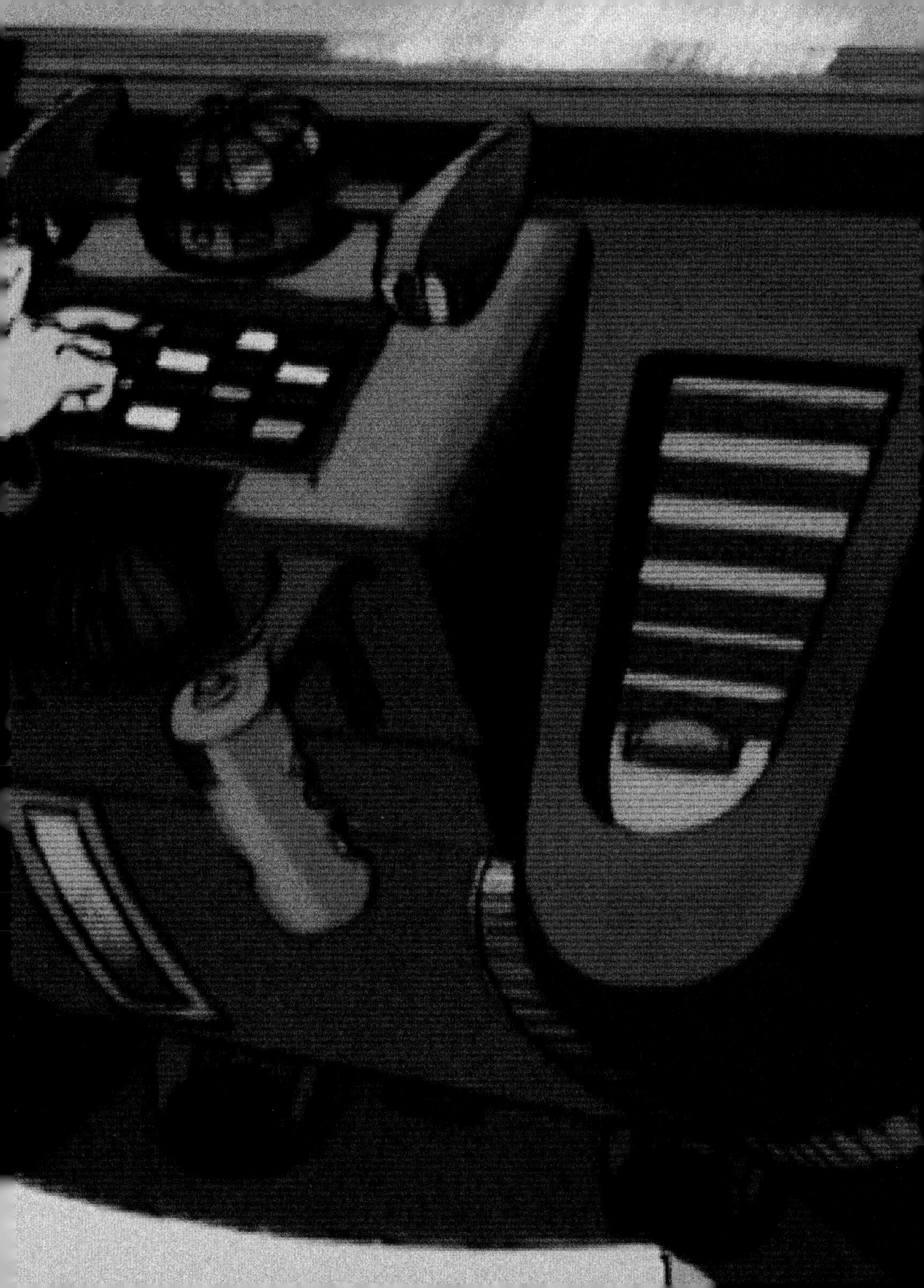

When planning any sort of group excursion, it makes sense to figure out all of the travel arrangements, including who's going with who, before you go—so you can either be in control or call shotgun.

Your masculinity
will be called into
question if you ask
for help. Never stop
to ask for directions.
Never read the instruc-
tions. Never follow the
recommended dosage.

Didn't read the book?

WHO CARES?

Your book club is filled with a bunch of whining privileged narcissists who couldn't tell a Franzen from a freeze-ray. If you don't like the book, don't read it—just go and gorge yourself on free wine and a selection of cheeses.

You deserve it.

Thanks and acknowledgments

IT TAKES A UNIVERSE TO PUBLISH A BOOK, and this one was no exception. I'm grateful to Alex Ward, Megan Startz, and all of the hardworking and dedicated folks at NBC Universal and Mattel for allowing me to frolic in the Eternian sunshine with my childhood chums. Special thanks must be given to Ed-It-Or (Jacob Lehman) and Dee-Zine-Or (Lynne Yeamans) and each and every Master at Universe Publishing. And a note to 12-year-old me, who I can see through the Time Corridor: You'll never need algebra. Just keep watching cartoons and playing with action figures and you'll be fine.

Author biographies

ROBB PEARLMAN IS A MASTER OF POP CULTURE. The author of more than twenty-five books for grown-ups and children, including *I Adulted, Star Trek: Fun with Kirk and Spock,* and *TV USA: An Atlas for Channel Surfers,* he watches a lot of television. A lot. He lives in New Jersey.

SKELETOR IS A MASTER OF EVIL, who is particularly interested in harnessing the power of Castle Grayskull for his own nefarious purposes. He lives on Eternia. This is his first book.

MASTERS
OF THE UNIVERSE

MASTERS
OF THE UNIVERSE